THIS SUPERHERO BOOK

BELONGS TO

_ _ _ _ _ _ _ _ _ _ _ _ _ _ _ _

(YOUR NAME)

AKA

_ _ _ _ _ _ _ _ _ _ _ _ _

(YOUR SUPERHERO NAME)

IF

FOUND, PLEASE RETURN TO

_ _ _ _ _ _ _ _ _ _ _ _ _ _ _ _

_ _ _ _ _ _ _ _ _ _ _ _ _ _ _ _

(ADDRESS)

FOR ARALI, ALFIE, KIT, AND JOE!

PUBLISHED IN 2013 BY

LAURENCE KING PUBLISHING LTD

361-373 CITY ROAD
LONDON EC1V 1LR
TEL + 44 20 7841 6900
FAX + 44 20 7841 6910
www.laurenceking.com
enquiries@laurenceking.com

REPRINTED 2013, 2014, 2015 (THREE TIMES), 2016

A CATALOGUE RECORD OF THIS BOOK IS AVAILABLE FROM
THE BRITISH LIBRARY.

ISBN 978-1-78067-3-059

DESIGNED BY JASON GODFREY
www.godfreydesign.co.uk

PRINTED IN CHINA

THE SUPER BOOK FOR SUPER-HEROES

JASON FORD

LAURENCE KING

UNCH!
OAR!!
ZZZTTTT
FOOF!
WOMP
OOOOMM!!
ROK!
SPLANG!
BAM!
SKWEE
SKWEEEP!
M!!
TZAM
FWOM!
THUD!
ZZOORCH!
OOM!
THOOM!
UNCH!

OOOSH!

OK!

SO YOU WANT TO DRAW
SUPERHEROES DOING
THINGS LIKE FLYING AND
FIGHTING SUPERVILLAINS.

ALL YOU NEED ARE SOME
PENCILS AND PENS
AND YOUR VERY OWN
SUPERPOWER...

?!

!!!

YOUR IMAGINATION!

LET'S DRAW A SUPERHERO

FOLLOW THESE SEVEN SIMPLE STEPS TO DRAW YOUR OWN SUPERHERO CHARACTER!

QUIFF (OPTIONAL)

ATHLETIC ARMS + LEGS

WIDE SHOULDERS

READY FOR ACTION POSE

BODY IS TRIANGULAR SHAPED

HERE'S HOW

① START WITH THE HEAD

② ADD THE BODY

③

FISTS EITHER SIDE OF WAIST

④ ADD ARMS

⑤

DRAW UPPER LEGS

⑥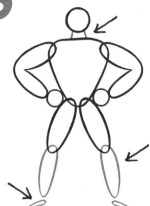

NECK, LOWER LEGS, & FEET

⑦

ADD DETAILS
FACE, HAIR
CLOAK, BELT,
LOGO, ETC

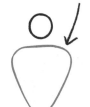
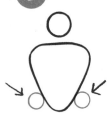
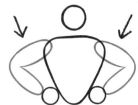

PRACTICE DRAWING
HERE

PRACTICE DRAWING
HERE

LET'S DRAW A COSTUME

A SUPERHERO NEEDS A COOL-LOOKING OUTFIT.

HERE ARE THE KEY PIECES TO CONSIDER WHEN DESIGNING YOUR COSTUME...

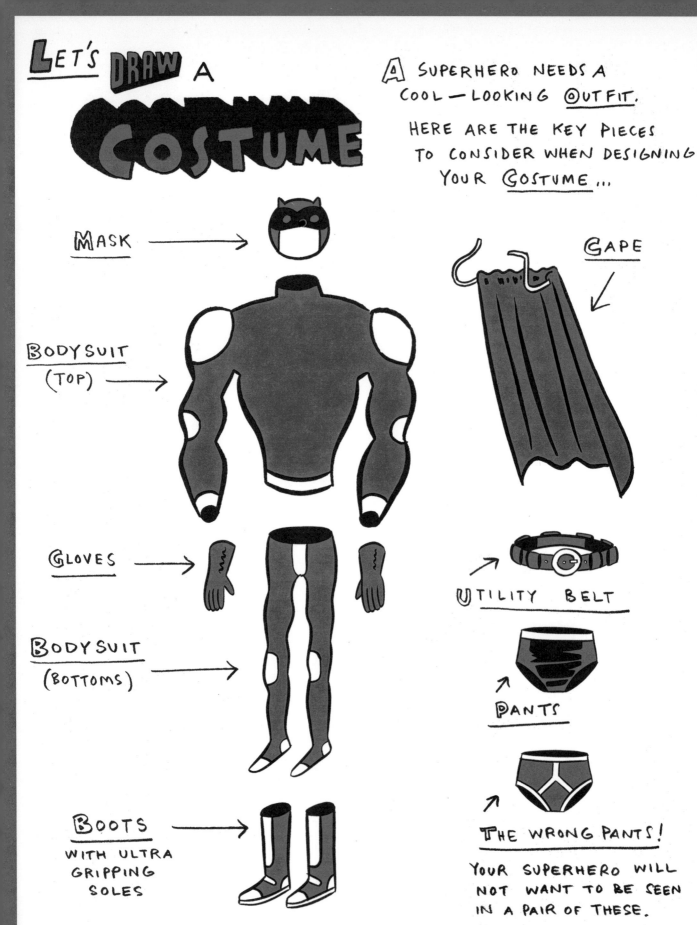

MASK ——→

CAPE

BODYSUIT (TOP) ——→

GLOVES ——→

UTILITY BELT

BODYSUIT (BOTTOMS) ——→

PANTS

THE WRONG PANTS!

YOUR SUPERHERO WILL NOT WANT TO BE SEEN IN A PAIR OF THESE.

BOOTS ——→
WITH ULTRA GRIPPING SOLES

A COOL COSTUME MAKES YOUR SUPERHERO IMMEDIATELY RECOGNIZABLE AND ALSO CONCEALS THEIR TRUE IDENTITY.

HAVE A GO AT <u>DRAWING</u> AN OUTFIT FOR THESE FIGURES BELOW.

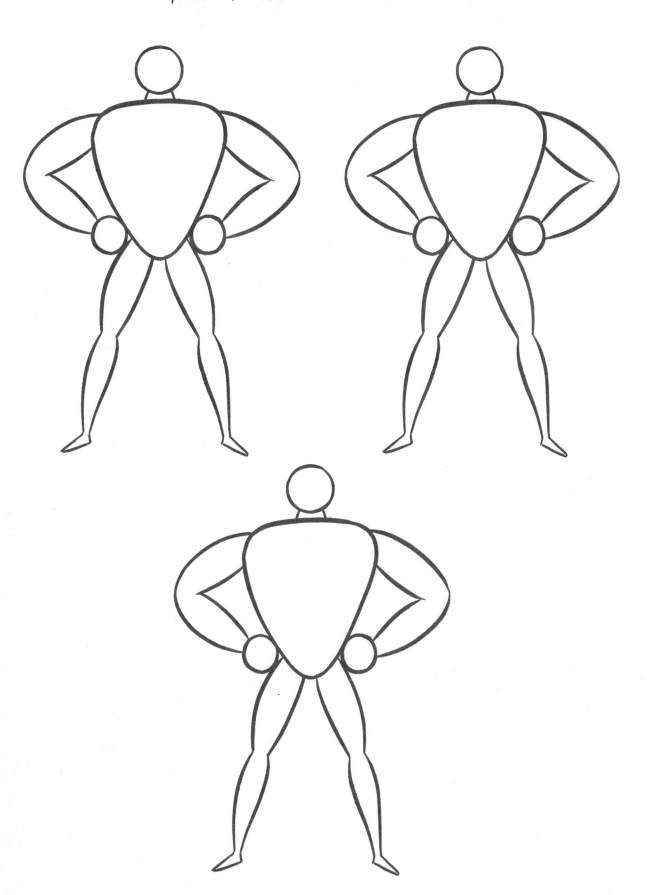

<u>U</u>SE DIFFERENT <u>COLORS</u>

FISTS ARE SIMILAR SIZE →

HEAD & BODY ARE LEANING FORWARD ←

NOTE RIGHT ARM & LEFT LEG ARE BEHIND →

NOTE LEFT ARM & RIGHT LEG ARE FORWARD ←

LET'S DRAW A SUPERHERO RUNNING

HERE'S HOW

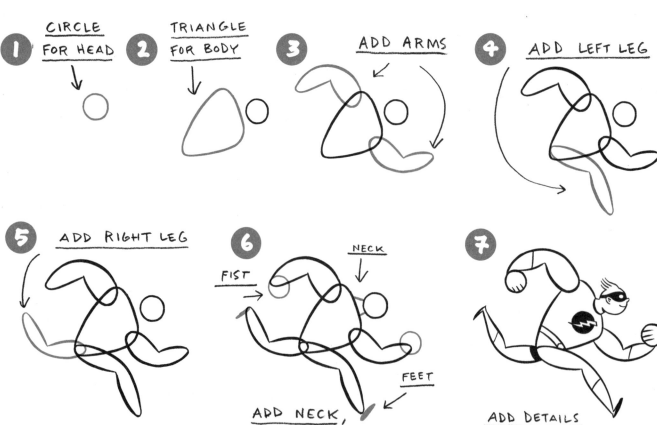

1 CIRCLE FOR HEAD ↓

2 TRIANGLE FOR BODY ↓

3 ADD ARMS

4 ADD LEFT LEG

5 ADD RIGHT LEG

6 NECK / FIST → / FEET → / ADD NECK, FISTS, & FEET

7 ADD DETAILS FACE, MASK, HAIR, BELT, LOGO, ETC...

PRACTICE DRAWING
HERE

PRACTICE DRAWING
HERE

 CAN RUN VERY FAST!

DRAW THE DIFFERENT
THINGS THAT THIS HERO
IS FASTER THAN.

 ARE VERY AGILE!

HE'S JUMPING OVER SOMETHING VERY TALL. WHAT IS IT?

 ARE VERY STRONG!

WHAT HEAVY OBJECT HAS THIS HERO STOPPED FROM CRASHING TO THE GROUND?

DRAW IT AND COLOR IT IN.

DRAW A **SPEEDING OBJECT** THAT OUR HERO HAS STOPPED WITH HIS SUPER STRENGTH!

LET'S DRAW A SUPER HERO

RUNNING TOWARDS YOU

THE FIST IS BIGGER THAN THE HEAD

THE HEAD SET LOW ON THE SHOULDERS

THIS FIST IS MUCH SMALLER THAN THE HEAD

TRIANGULAR SHAPED BODY

THIS FOOT IS LARGER

THIS FOOT IS SMALLER. IT'S FURTHEST AWAY FROM YOU

HERE'S HOW

1 CIRCLE FOR HEAD

2 TRIANGLE FOR BODY

3 LONG LEFT ARM

4 SHORT RIGHT ARM

5 DRAW LEGS

SMALL LEFT LEG (THIGH)

LONG RIGHT LEG (COMING FORWARD)

6 HANDS & FEET

7 ADD DETAILS

FACE, HAIR, CLOAK, BELT, LOGO, ETC...

PRACTICE DRAWING
HERE

THIS HERO'S SPECIAL POWER IS

THIS HERO'S SPECIAL POWER IS ELASTICITY!

JOIN UP HIS **HEAD**, **HANDS**, AND **FEET** WITH A VERY **BENDY BODY**

HOW TO DRAW SOMEONE WHO IS

INVISIBLE

USE A DOTTED LINE

BEFORE

AFTER

ALSO GOOD FOR DRAWING FORCE FIELDS

WITHOUT A FORCEFIELD

WITH A FORCE FIELD

DRAW AN <u>INVISIBLE CHARACTER</u>
INSIDE A <u>FORCE FIELD</u>
HERE

THERE ARE INVISIBLE SUPERHEROES

IN THE ROOM. BUT <u>WHERE</u> ARE THEY?

DRAW THEM FIGHTING THESE <u>CRIMINALS</u>!

LET'S DRAW A SUPER HERO

FLYING TOWARDS YOU

THIS FIST IS BIGGER THAN THE HEAD

BODY IS OVAL SHAPED

THIS FIST IS MUCH SMALLER THAN THE HEAD

THIS THIGH IS SMALLER

LARGER THIGH WITH SMALL FOOT

HERE'S HOW

1 START WITH THE HEAD

2 OVAL FOR THE BODY

3 DRAW THE ARMS

4 TWO MORE CIRCLES FOR FISTS

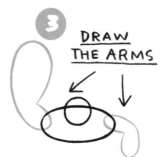

5 ADD THE LARGER THIGH

6 DRAW SMALL THIGH & FOOT

7 FINALLY ADD THE DETAILS

PRACTICE DRAWING
HERE

THIS HERO'S **SUPERPOWER** IS...

SUPERPOWER

He's a human flame thrower! Finish off the jets of flame. What's he scorching with his FIERY skills?

WHAT'S THE **MAD SCIENTIST** THINKING ABOUT?

THIS HERO'S **UNUSUAL POWER** IS...

ICE

FWOM!

COMPLETE THE ICY BLASTS COMING OUT OF HIS HANDS.

WHAT'S HE DOING WITH THEM? IS HE <u>FREEZING</u> SOMEONE OR SOMETHING?
COMPLETE THE FROSTY SCENE.

HERE'S A **HERO** FLYING ACROSS THE CITY!

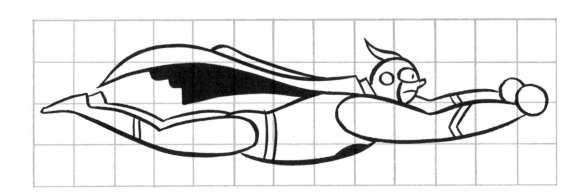

COMPLETE THE CITYSCAPE
WITH MORE BUILDINGS
AND SKYSCRAPERS.

PRACTICE DRAWING A FLYING SUPERHERO

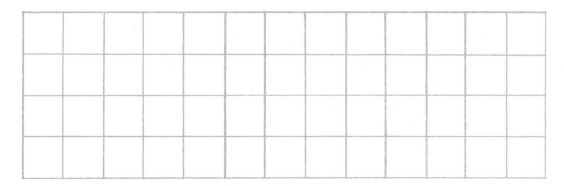

USE THE GRID TO COPY THE FIGURE

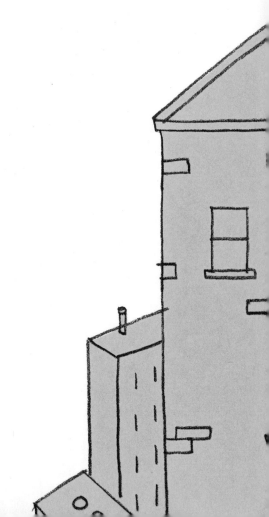

THIS HERO'S SUPERPOWER IS...

X-RAY VISION

WHAT CAN HE SEE INSIDE THE BUILDING?

WHAT'S THE VAN CARRYING? DRAW IT.

DRAW SOME MORE SKYSCRAPERS
AND COLOR THEM IN.

WHEN NOT BEING A <u>SUPERHERO</u>,
IT IS <u>VITAL</u> TO KEEP CRIME FIGHTING
ALTER-EGOS <u>TOP SECRET</u>!

WHO KNEW THAT YOUR
VERY OWN <u>GRANDMOTHER</u>
IS A **SUPERHERO**

SHE BECOMES...

AND YOUR FAMILY'S
PET DOG IS ONE TOO!
IT BECOMES...

WHAT'S **CLIMBING** UP THE BUILDING?

DRAW THE SUPERHEROES USING THEIR
SPECIAL POWERS AGAINST THE
GIANT FOE.

SWAMP CREATURE

FINISH OFF THIS SLIMY DRAWING
WITH A HEAD, BODY, & LEGS.

DESIGN & CREATE YOUR OWN MASKS!

THEY ARE PRE-CUT.
JUST POP THEM OUT
OF THE PAGE.

ATTACH STRING
OR ELASTIC
TO THESE HOLES
AND FASTEN.

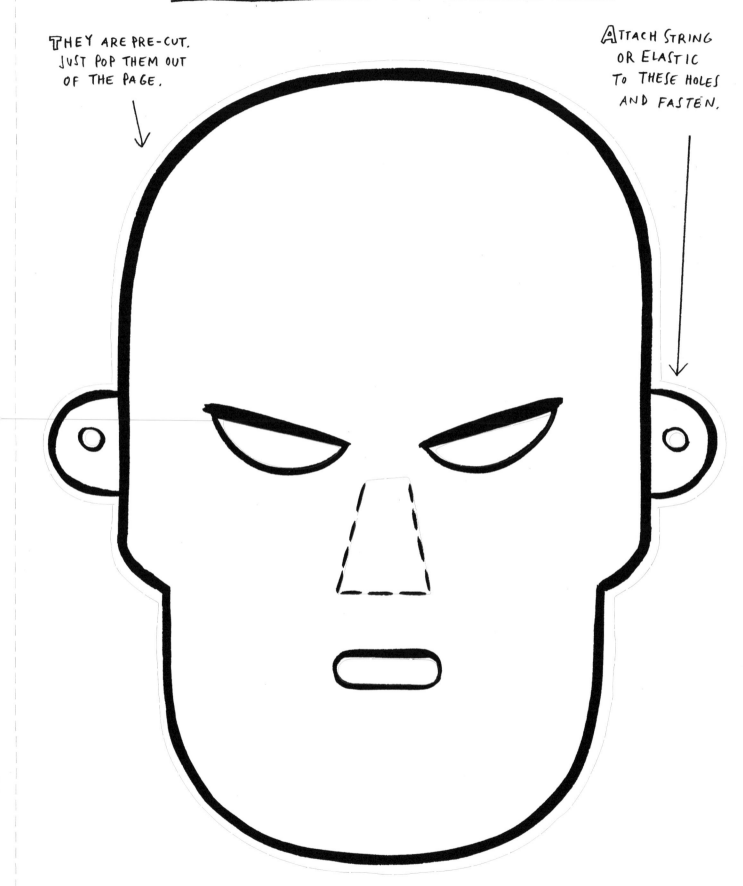

DECORATE YOUR MASKS BY ADDING COLOR, LETTERS, SYMBOLS
OR EXTRA PIECES (LIKE WINGS, FLAMES, ANTENNAE ETC...)

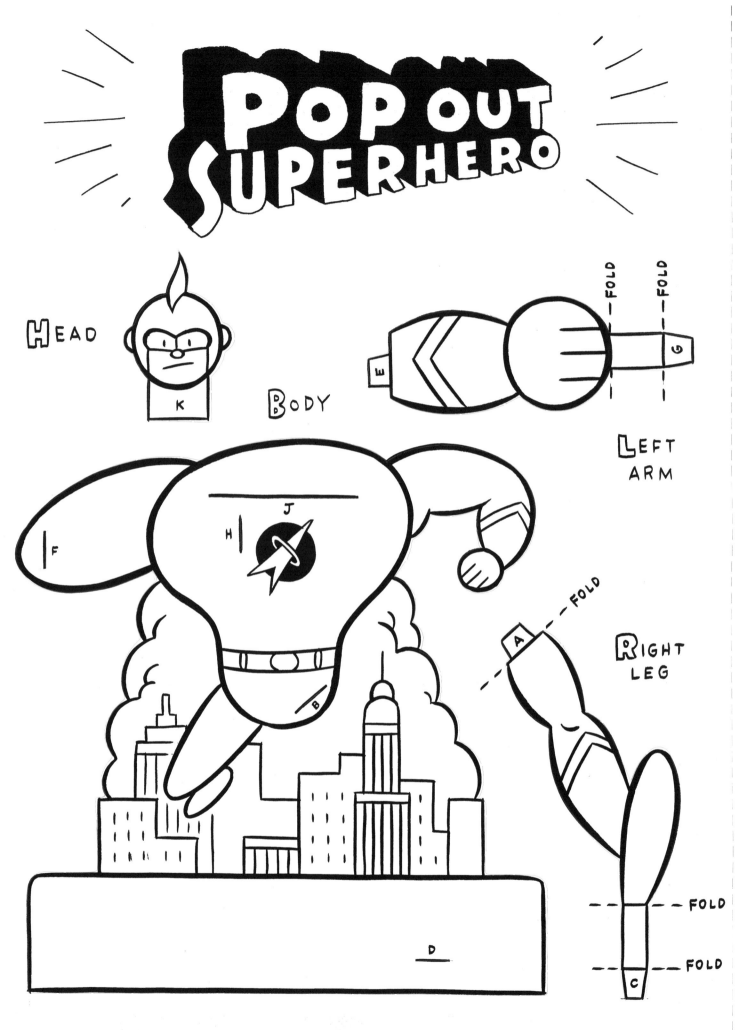

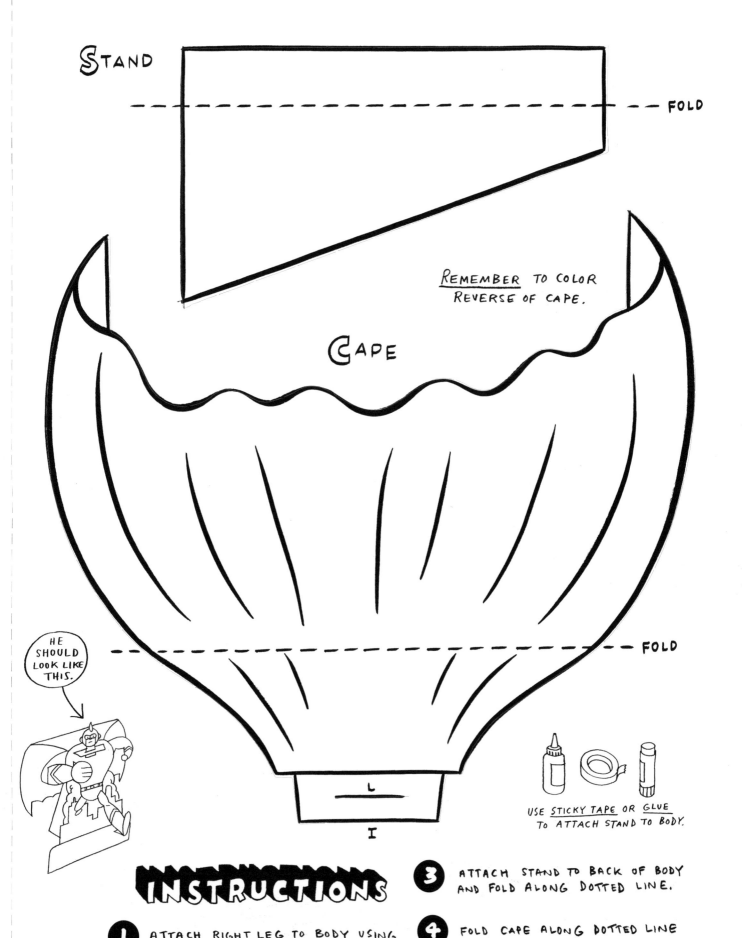

STAND

- - - FOLD

REMEMBER TO COLOR
REVERSE OF CAPE.

CAPE

HE
SHOULD
LOOK LIKE
THIS.

- - - FOLD

L

I

USE _STICKY TAPE_ OR _GLUE_
TO ATTACH STAND TO BODY.

INSTRUCTIONS

1 ATTACH RIGHT LEG TO BODY USING
FLAP 'A' / SLOT 'B' AND FLAP 'C' / SLOT 'D'

2 ATTACH LEFT ARM TO BODY USING
FLAP 'E' / SLOT 'F' AND FLAP 'G' / SLOT 'H'

3 ATTACH STAND TO BACK OF BODY
AND FOLD ALONG DOTTED LINE.

4 FOLD CAPE ALONG DOTTED LINE
AND ATTACH TO BODY USING
FLAP 'I' / SLOT 'J'.

5 ATTACH HEAD TO CAPE USING
FLAP 'K' / SLOT 'L'.

UH OH! LOOK OUT, IT'S THE

EVIL CLOWN

COMPLETE THIS DRAWING OF
AN EVIL CUSTARD PIE THROWING VILLAIN!

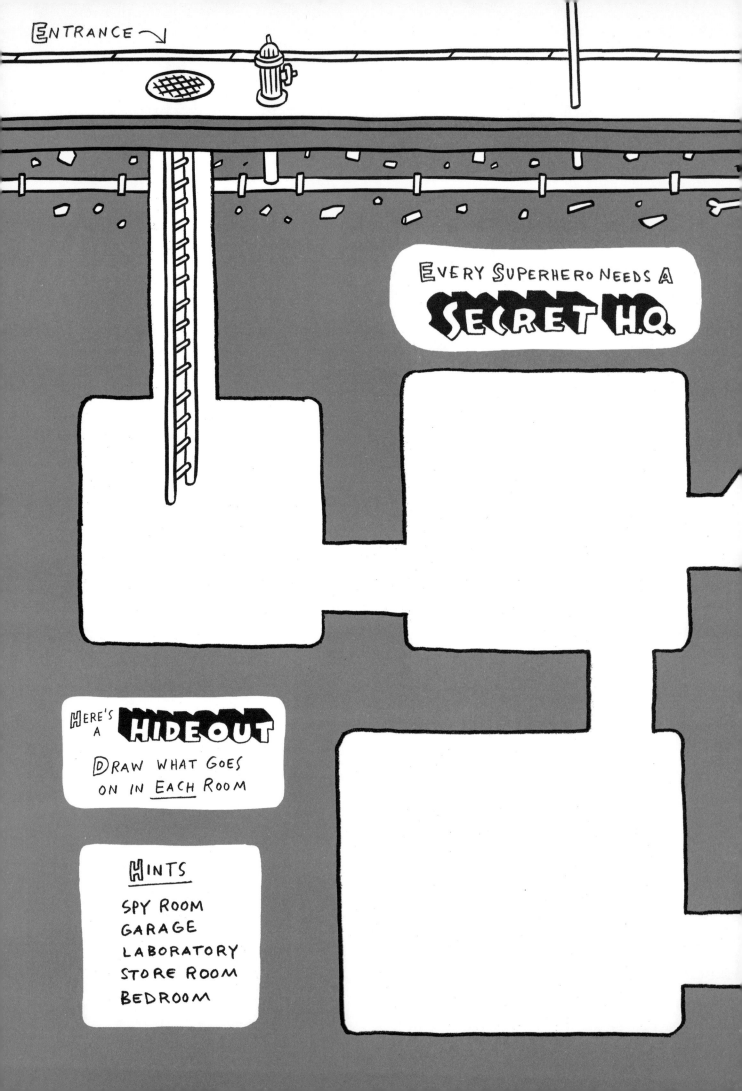

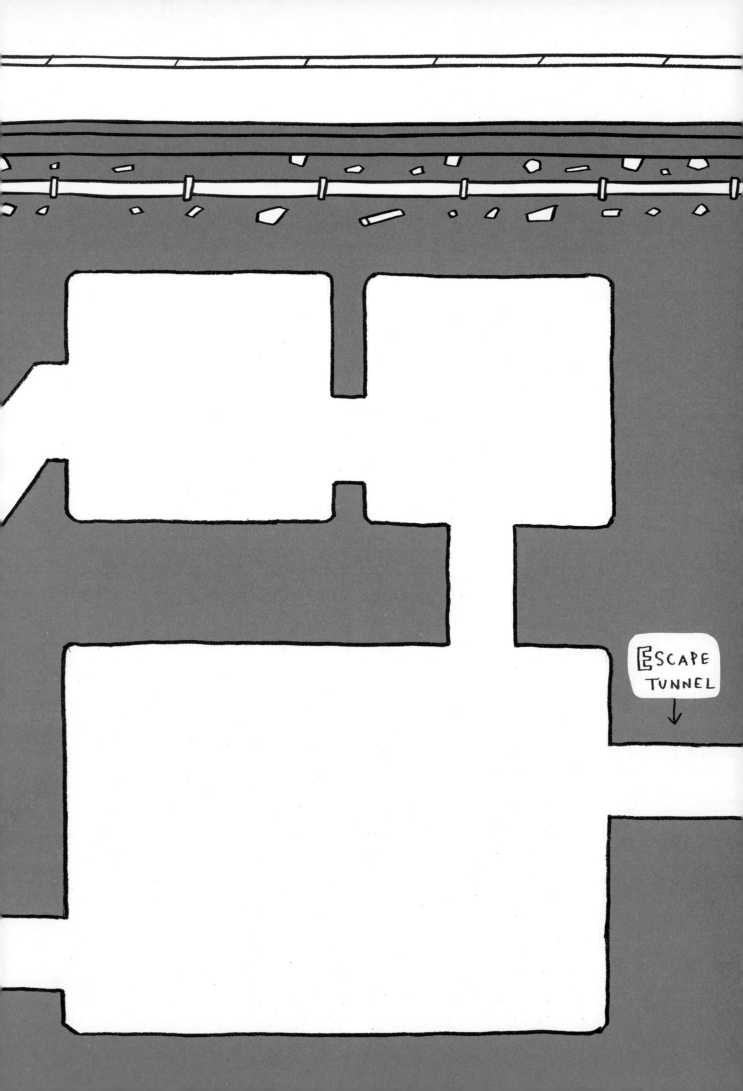

STANDARD UTILITY BELT

 **COLOR** IN THESE __COOL__ ITEMS

HOLES

GOOD FOR MAKING YOUR ESCAPE.

FORCE FIELD ANORAK

REPELS ALL TYPES OF BEAMS AND BLASTS.

IMMOBILIZING GUNK

STOPS VILLAINS IN THEIR TRACKS!

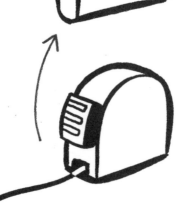

SMOKE BOMBS

CREATE A DENSE SCREEN INSTANTLY. TOTALLY DISORIENTATING!

GRAPPLE HOOK
WITH 50 METERS OF HIGH TENSION WIRE

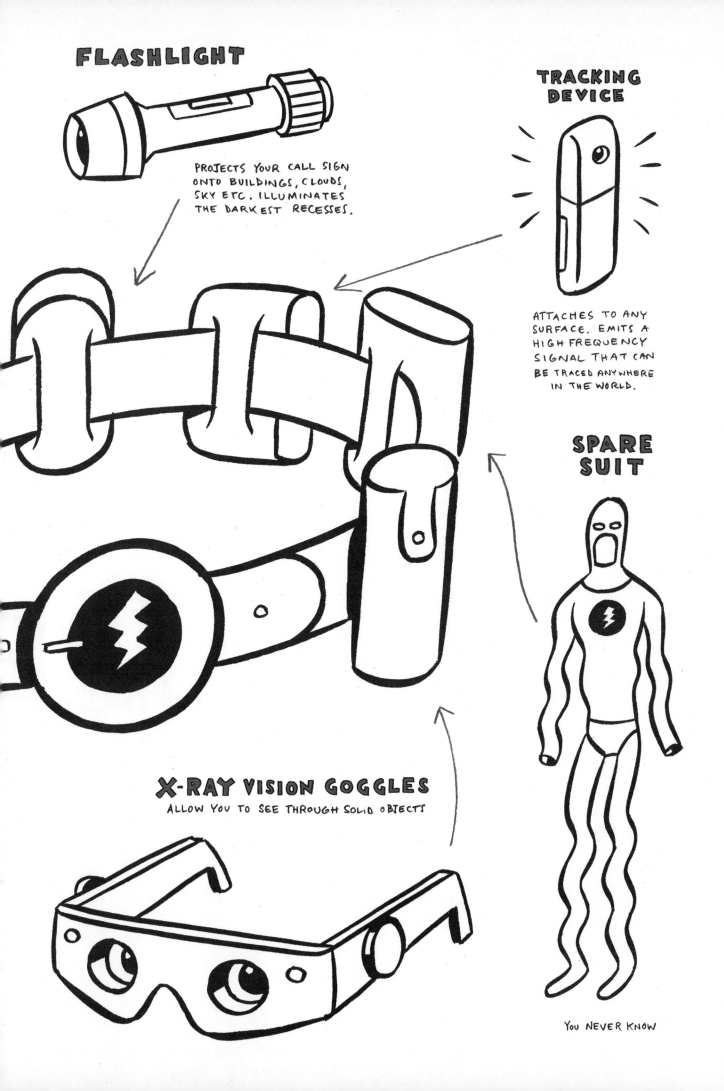

FLASHLIGHT

PROJECTS YOUR CALL SIGN ONTO BUILDINGS, CLOUDS, SKY ETC. ILLUMINATES THE DARKEST RECESSES.

TRACKING DEVICE

ATTACHES TO ANY SURFACE. EMITS A HIGH FREQUENCY SIGNAL THAT CAN BE TRACED ANYWHERE IN THE WORLD.

SPARE SUIT

X-RAY VISION GOGGLES

ALLOW YOU TO SEE THROUGH SOLID OBJECTS

YOU NEVER KNOW

CUSTOMIZED UTILITY BELT

DRAW THE THINGS YOU WOULD HAVE ON YOUR BELT.

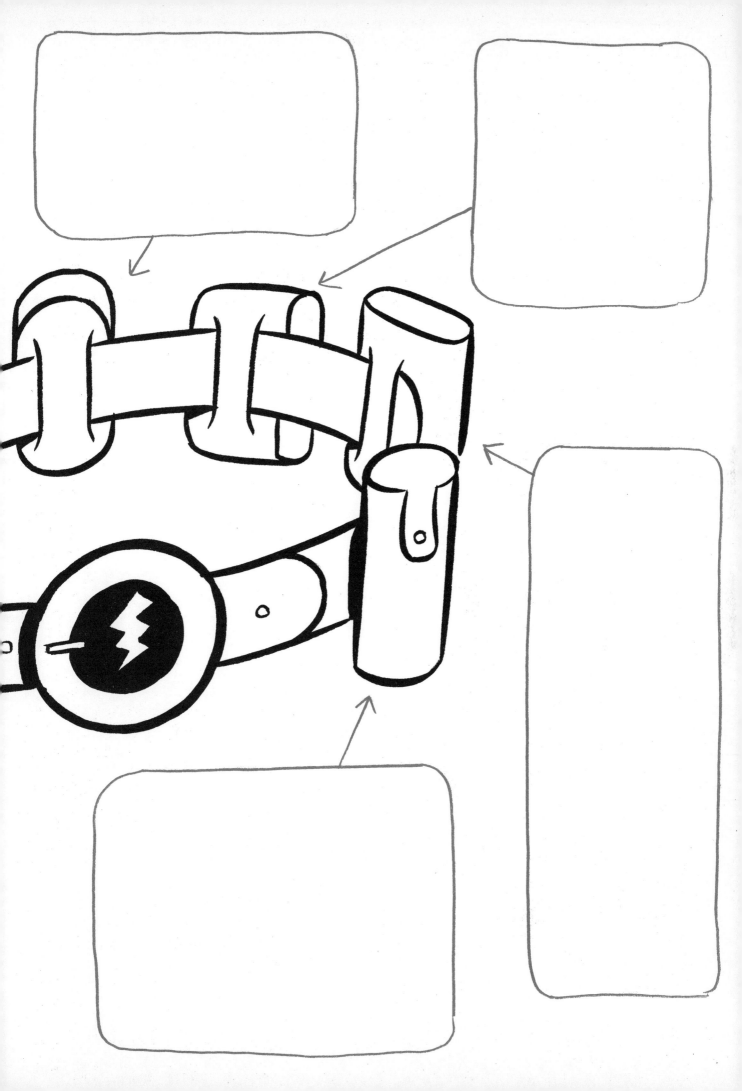

COMPLETE THESE CHARACTERS.
DRAW HEADS, ARMS, BODIES, & LEGS.
ARE THEY GOOD GUYS OR BAD GUYS?

THE HUMAN FLY

HERO   YES ☐   NO ☐
VILLAIN YES ☐   NO ☐

SPECIAL POWERS _ _ _ _ _ _ _ _ _ _ _ _ _ _ _ _

ROBOMAN

HERO   YES ☐ NO ☐   SPECIAL
                        POWERS _ _ _ _ _ _ _ _ _ _ _
VILLAIN YES ☐ NO ☐
                        _ _ _ _ _ _ _ _ _ _ _ _

SPACE BEAST

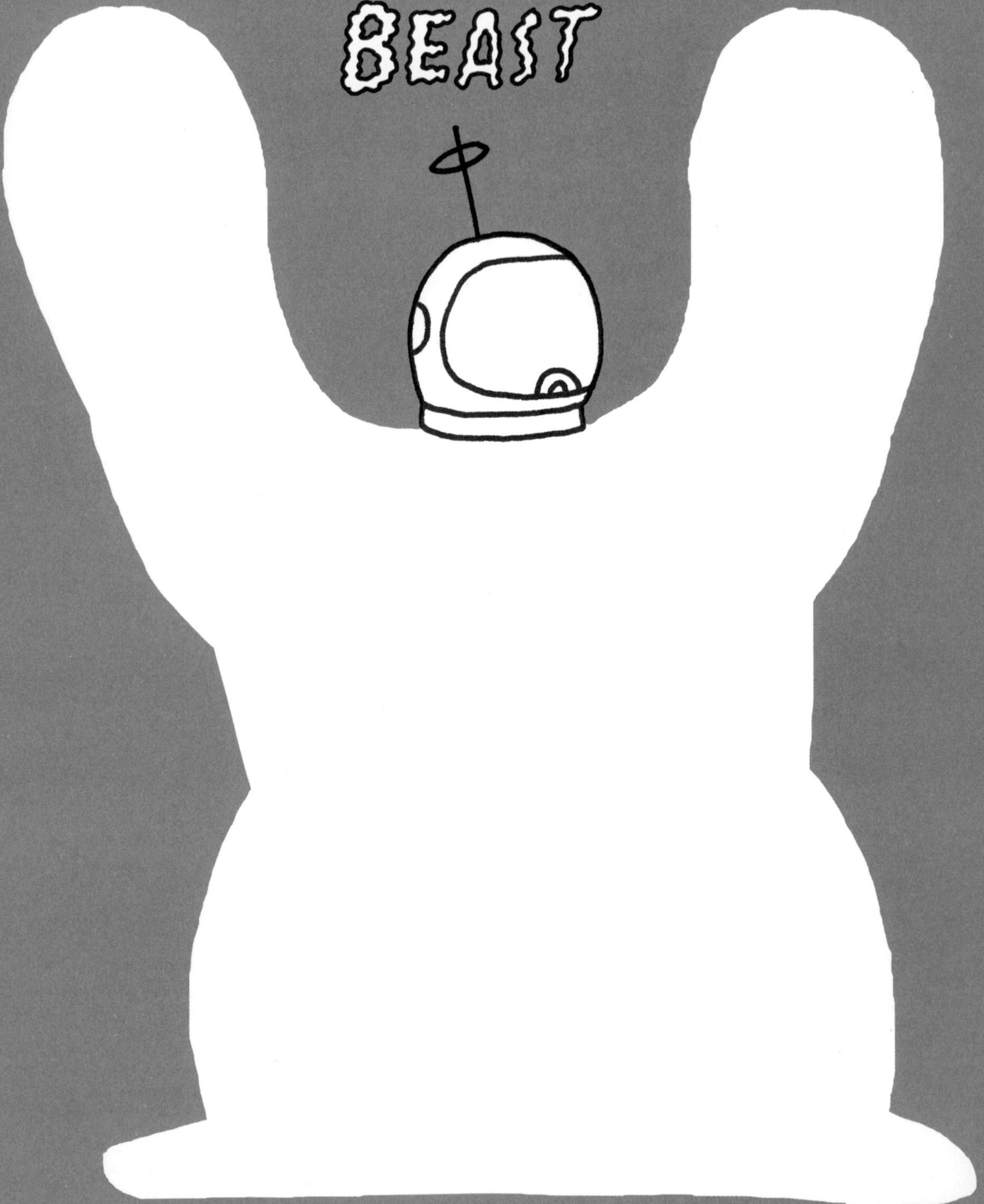

HERO

	YES	NO
	☐	☐

VILLAIN

	YES	NO
	☐	☐

SPECIAL POWERS _____

_____

LIZARD
boy

HERO
VILLAIN

YES ☐ NO ☐
YES ☐ NO ☐

SPECIAL
POWERS _ _ _ _ _ _ _ _ _
_ _ _ _ _ _ _ _ _ _ _ _ _

LET'S DRAW YOUR OWN
SUPER CAR

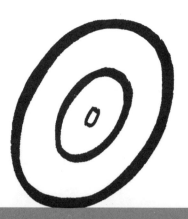

TECHNICAL DATA	
TOP SPEED	
ENGINE SIZE	
FUEL TYPE	
SPECIAL FEATURES	

LET'S DRAW SOME MORE  SUPER CARS
STARTING WITH THESE <u>WHEELS</u>.

BAAROOM!

VAROOOM!

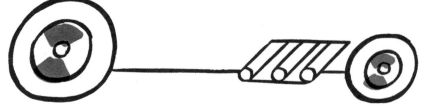

GIVE EACH CAR DIFFERENT <u>SECRET WEAPONS</u>.

VAROOM!

BAAROOM!

HAHAHAHA!

WHAT SECRET GADGETS WILL YOU GIVE YOUR VILLAIN'S CAR?

SEND SECRET MESSAGES

To YOUR SUPERHERO PALS USING THIS <u>SECRET CODE WHEEL</u>

WHAT YOU WILL NEED TO MAKE YOUR SECRET CODE WHEEL ...

<u>SCISSORS</u>   <u>PENCIL</u>

How To Make

1 CAREFULLY CUT OUT <u>BOTH</u> WHEELS WITH THE SCISSORS.

2 GENTLY PUSH SHARP END OF PENCIL THROUGH THE <u>CENTRE</u> OF EACH WHEEL (BLACK DOT).

3 PLACE THE SMALLER WHEEL ON TOP OF THE LARGER WHEEL SO THE 2 HOLES ARE <u>ALIGNED</u>.

4 PUSH THE PENCIL THROUGH <u>BOTH</u> WHEELS SO THAT YOU CAN ROTATE THE SMALLER WHEEL.

How To Use

1 CHOOSE WHERE YOU WANT TO POSITION LETTER 'A' ON THE <u>SMALLER</u> WHEEL WITH A LETTER ON THE <u>LARGER</u> WHEEL.

2 FOR EXAMPLE — ALIGN 'A' WITH 'Q' AND 'B' BECOMES 'R', 'C' BECOMES 'S' AND SO ON.

3 USING THIS CODE, REVEAL THE SECRET MESSAGE <u>BELOW</u>...

"CUUJ QJ IUSHUJ XG CYTDYWXJ"

<u>NOW YOU'RE READY!</u>

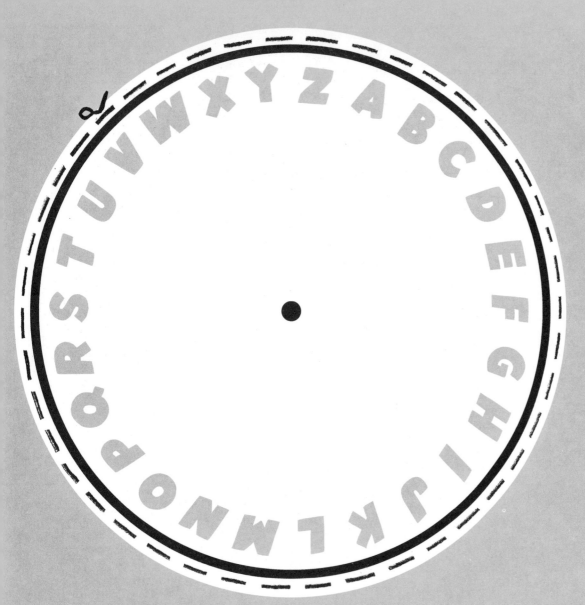

SUPER
HERO
SECRET CODE WHEEL

BELONGS TO

SUPERHERO NAME

WHO'S THE **HERO** FIGHTING WITH?
DRAW SOMEONE OR <u>SOMETHING.</u>

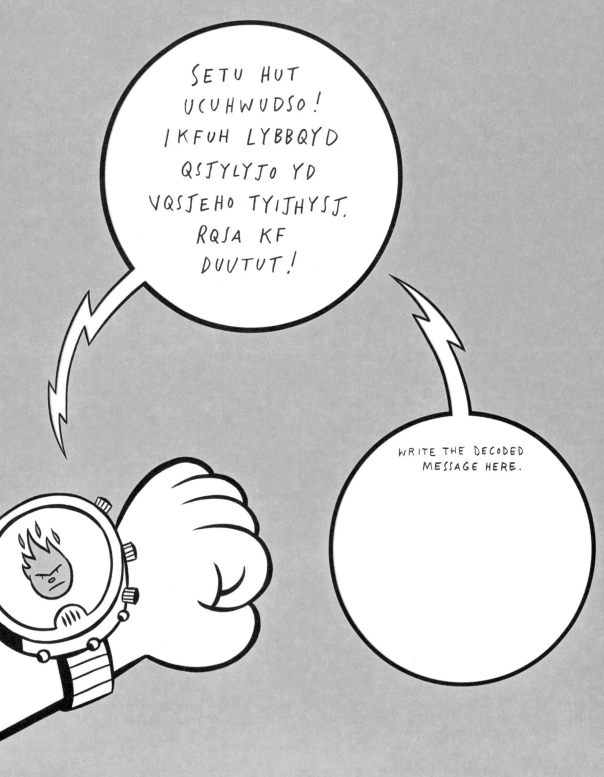

WHAT'S HE **RUNNING** FROM? FALLING BUILDING?
GIANT HAND?
FLYING EVIL ROBOT?
EXPLOSION?

LET'S TAKE A CLOSER LOOK
WITH THE **X-RAY VISION**

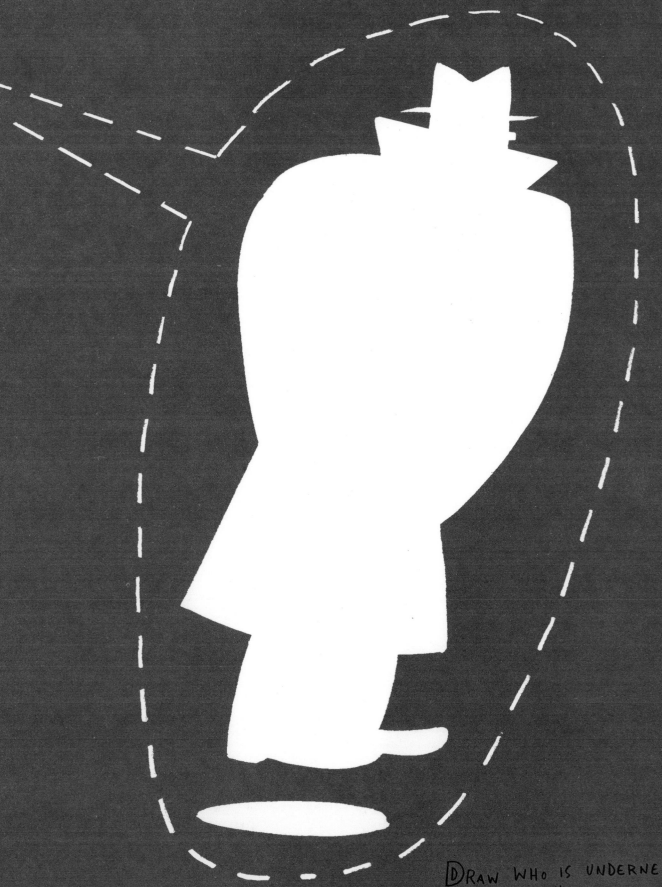

DRAW WHO IS UNDERNEATH
THE HAT & COAT.

THIS HERO CAN **TIME TRAVEL!**

HE'S TRAVELED BACK TO THE TIME OF THE **DINOSAURS!**

HERE ARE SOME IDEAS FOR YOU TO DRAW TO COMPLETE THE PREHISTORIC SCENE...

PTERODACTYLS

SWAMP

STRANGE PLANTS

DINOSAURS

HE CAN ALSO

TIME TRAVEL

INTO THE **FUTURE!**

THE YEAR **4013** TO BE PRECISE.

HERE ARE SOME _IDEAS_ FOR YOU TO _DRAW_
TO COMPLETE THE FUTURISTIC SCENE ...

SKYSCRAPERS

SPACE CRAFT

HIGHWAYS
IN THE SKY

ROBOTS

LET'S DRAW A HOUSE FOR A SUPERHERO

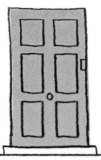

LET'S DRAW A HOUSE FOR A SUPERVILLAIN

RAYGUNS

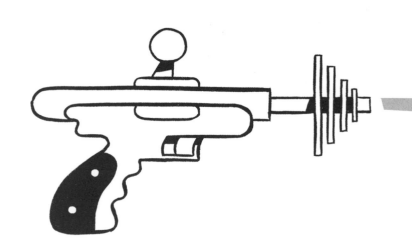

At times, there's nothing more handy than a ray gun to ZZAP, STUN, IMMOBILIZE, or simply VAPORIZE A FOE!

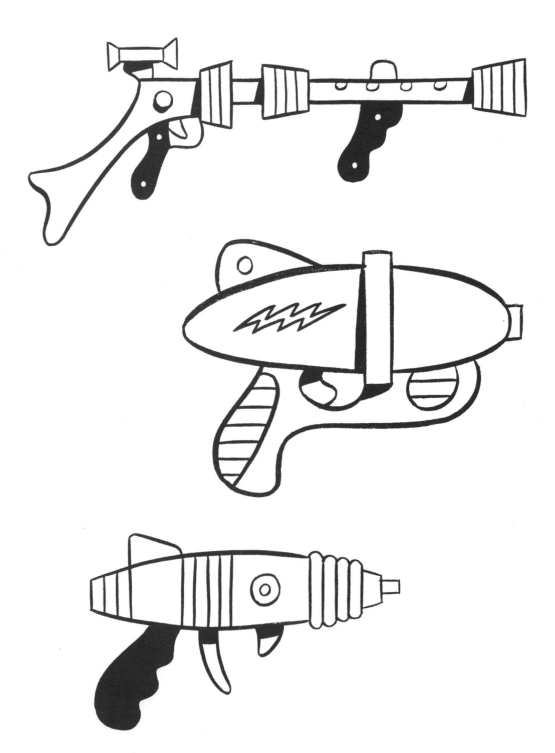

DRAW SOME RAYS FOR THESE GUNS. WHAT DOES EACH RAY DO?

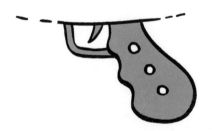

WHAT **POWER** DOES EACH RAYGUN HAVE ?

ABOVE the CITY
a BATTLE
RAGES

----- VERSUS -----

SUPERHERO   **SUPERVILLAIN**

DRAW YOUR SUPERHERO USING THEIR SPECIAL
POWERS TO <u>DEFEAT</u> A DASTARDLY VILLAIN!

A SECRET ISLAND H.Q.

WHAT'S GOING ON _INSIDE_ THIS ROCKY OUTCROP?

SHH! IT'S A _SECRET H.Q._!

DRAW YOUR SUPERHERO
USING HIS SECRET BASE
AND FINISH NAMING THE
DIFFERENT ROOMS.

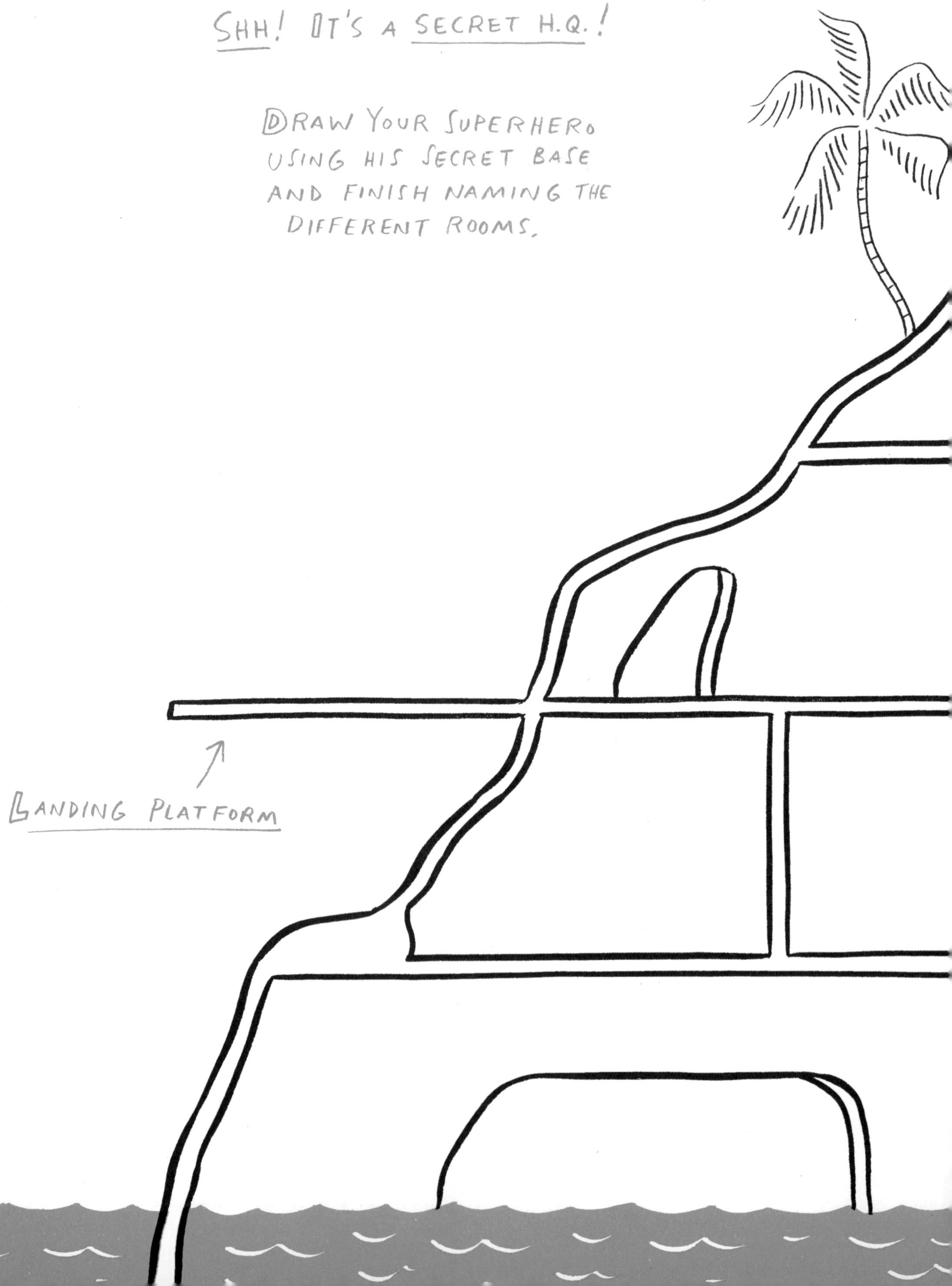

LANDING PLATFORM

AIR VENT
↓

RADAR AND
GPS AERIAL
←

ESCAPE ROUTE
↓

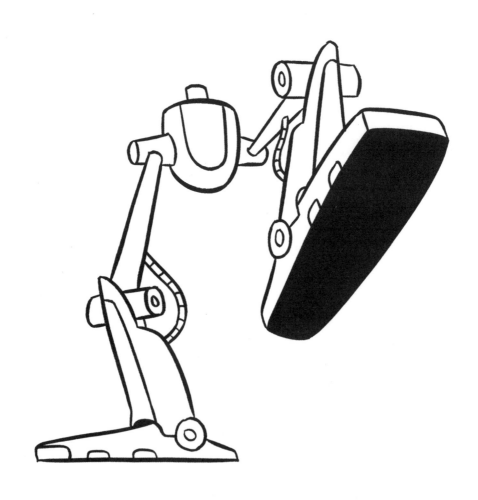

GIVE THIS ROBOT A BODY, ARMS, & A HEAD.
IT'S RAMPAGING THROUGH THE CITY. DRAW SOME BUILDINGS BEING CRUSHED!

HERE COMES ANOTHER FLYING OVERHEAD.

DRAW A BODY AND SHOW HOW IT'S FLYING OVER THE CITY.

An IMPORTANT PART OF A
SUPERHERO'S ARSENAL—

THE

COLOR THEM IN!

FLAME THROWER
EXHAUST

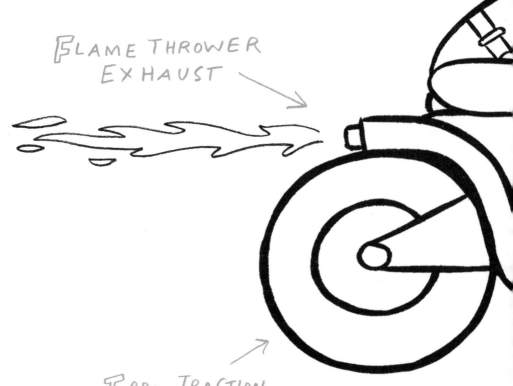

TURBO TRACTION
TIRES

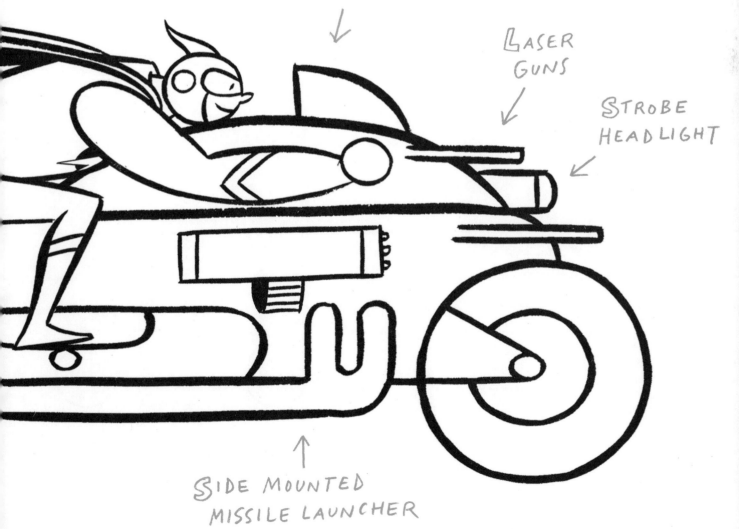

BULLET PROOF
WINDSHIELD

LASER
GUNS

STROBE
HEADLIGHT

SIDE MOUNTED
MISSILE LAUNCHER

LET'S DRAW A SUPER BIKE

1 DRAW TWO PAIRS OF
CIRCLES FOR WHEELS
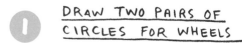

2 OBLONG FOR
BODY
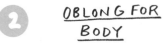
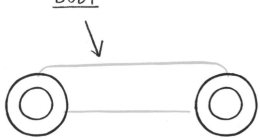

3 GAS TANK
& WINDSHIELD

4 ADD EXHAUST
PIPE
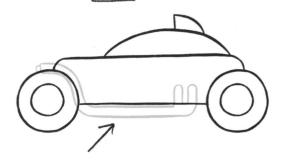

5 AND LASER GUNS,
HEADLIGHT, AND
BODY DETAILS
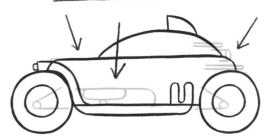

6 AND FINALLY, THE
MISSILE LAUNCHER
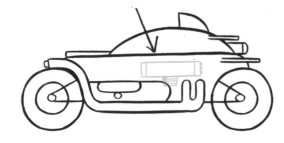

PRACTICE DRAWING
A SUPERBIKE HERE

LET'S DRAW SOME MORE SUPERBIKES

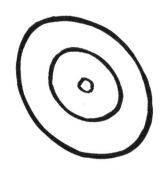

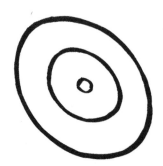

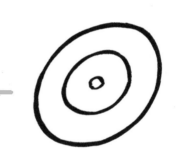

HAHAHAHA!

WHAT EVIL EXTRAS DOES IT HAVE?

DRAW A SUPERHERO'S **SUB-AQUATIC H.Q.**
ON THE ⊚CEAN FLOOR. HOW WOULD IT LOOK?

DRAW

A MAP

OF YOUR NEIGHBORHOOD

IF YOU WERE A **SUPERHERO** WHERE WOULD YOUR SECRET H.Q. BE? WHERE WOULD YOU BATTLE YOUR **FOES**?

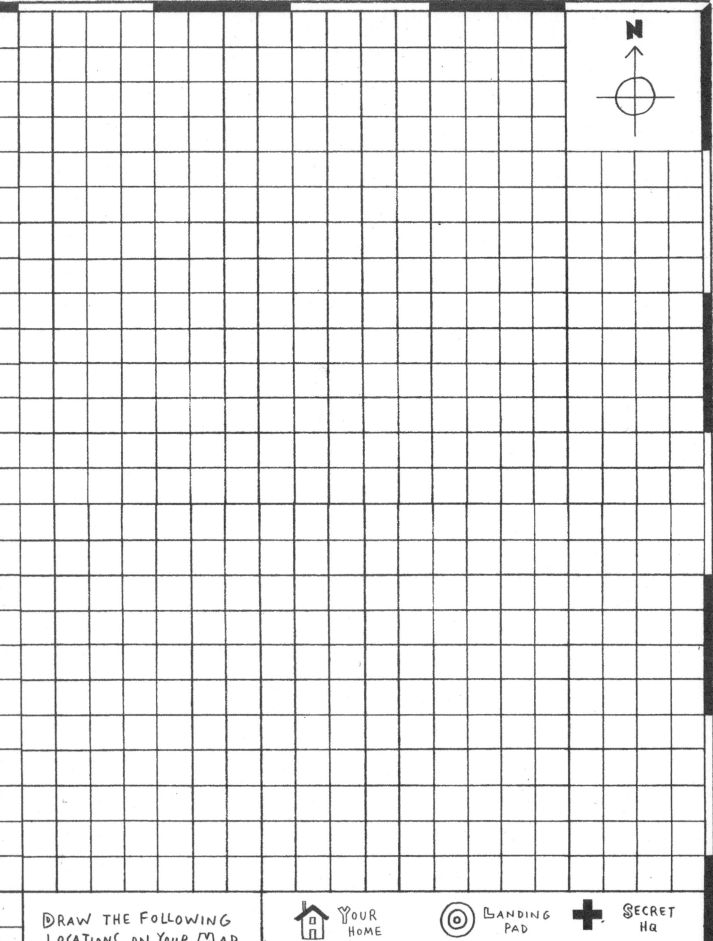

DRAW THE FOLLOWING LOCATIONS ON YOUR MAP USING DIFFERENT COLORS

YOUR HOME

SUPERHERO ACTIVITY

LANDING PAD

TIME PORTAL

SECRET HQ

VILLAIN ACTIVITY

THE ADVENTURES OF _____ *

in "THE DOOMSDAY MACHINE"

DRAW YOUR OWN COMIC STRIP! JUST FOLLOW THE CAPTIONS TO CREATE THE ACTION!

* YOUR SUPERHERO

① OUR HERO IS FLYING OVER THE CITY...

SUDDENLY A STRANGE RAY COMES FROM THE SKY!

② IT'S ENCASED THE CITY IN ICE!

WHERE IS THE RAY COMING FROM?

A STRANGE SPACECRAFT ABOVE THE EARTH!

ABOARD THE CRAFT... A DOOMSDAY MACHINE.

IT'S THE MAD SCIENTIST!

HE ORDERS HIS EVIL ROBOT TO ATTACK.

OUR HERO IS TRAPPED IN THE ROBOT'S HAND!

...BUT MANAGES TO ACTIVATE HIS SMART WATCH.

THE WATCH EMITS A SIGNAL THAT ALLOWS OUR HERO TO CONTROL THE ROBOT.

THE ROBOT DESTROYS THE DOOMSDAY MACHINE WITH A LOUD EXPLOSION!!

OUR HERO CAPTURES THE MAD SCIENTIST...

...AND SAVES THE WORLD!

THE END

THE **VILLAIN'S** HIDE OUT
HAS BEEN <u>DISCOVERED</u>.

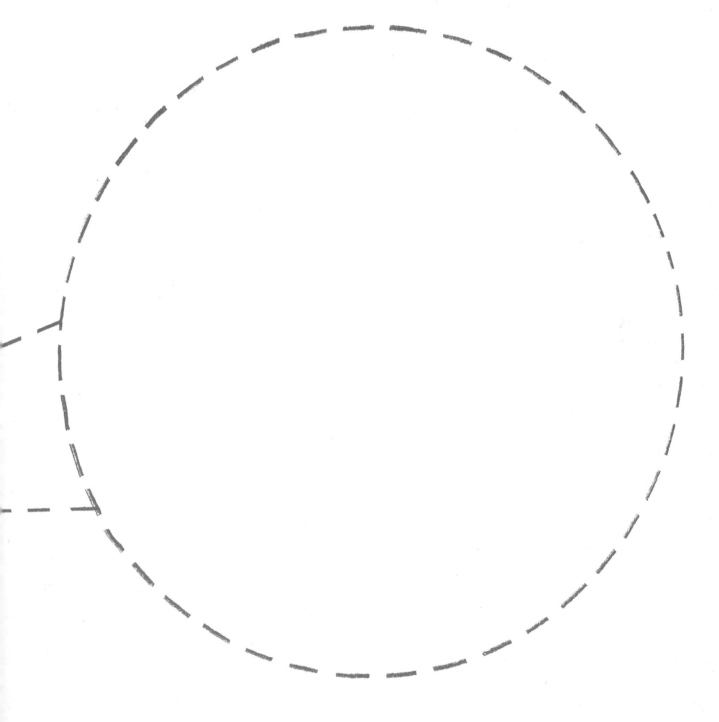

WHAT CAN THE SUPERHERO
SEE THROUGH THE <u>KEYHOLE</u>?

CREATE YOUR OWN

SUPERHERO GLOVES

1 DRAW AROUND YOUR <u>HANDS</u> SO THEY JOIN ONTO THE <u>CUFFS</u> BELOW.

2 NOW INSIDE THEM, DRAW THE <u>SECRET WEAPON</u> THAT IS CONCEALED IN EACH <u>SUPERHERO GLOVE</u>.

LEFT

DRAW A SUPER FLYING MACHINE
SO OUR HERO CAN ZOOM ACROSS THE SKY.

WHOOOSH!

FILL IN THE INFORMATION SHEET

TECHNICAL DATA	
TOP SPEED	
ENGINE SIZE	
FUEL TYPE	
SPECIAL FEATURES	

HERE'S THE
SUPER FLYING MACHINE
COCKPIT
WARNING! ALIEN CRAFT APPROACHING
FINISH THE CONTROL PANEL BY ADDING MORE BUTTONS & DIALS.
MISSILES

LABEL EACH BUTTON & DIAL SO OUR HERO KNOWS WHAT THEY DO.

FUEL

WHO IS THIS **SINISTER** CHARACTER
IN HIS COCKPIT? DRAW AN ALIEN CRAFT FOR HIM.

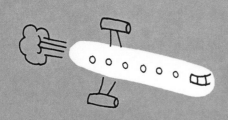 DRAW MORE **FLYING MACHINES**

USE THESE SHAPES TO CREATE MORE **SUPERHERO** AIRCRAFT.

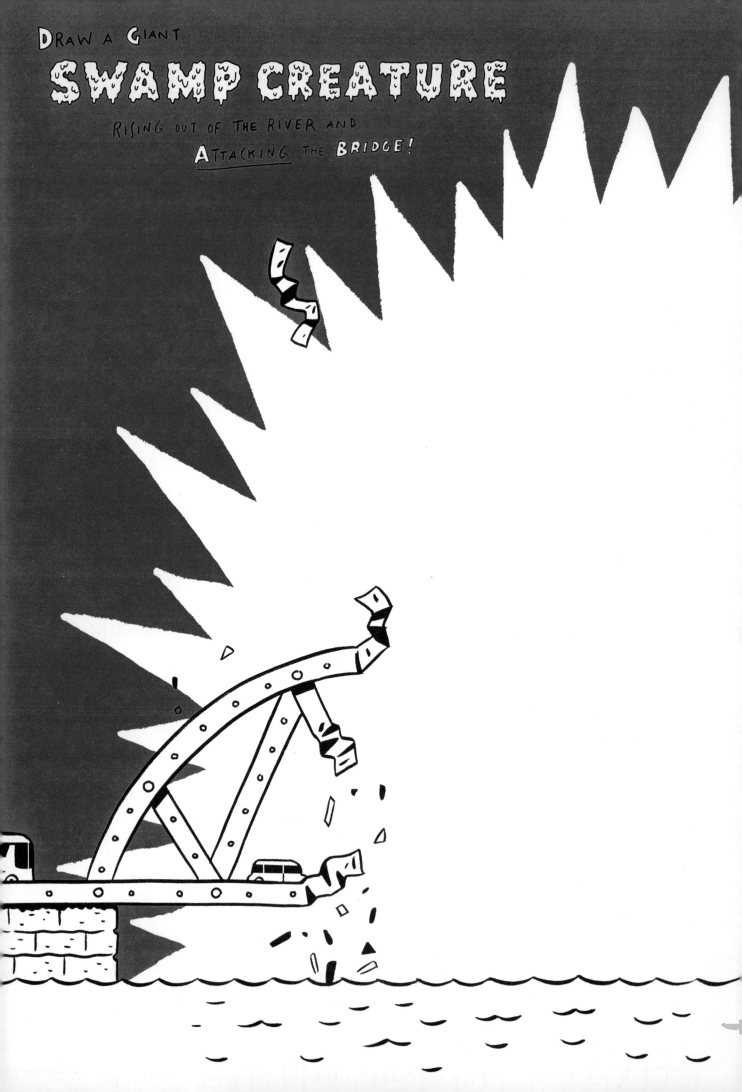

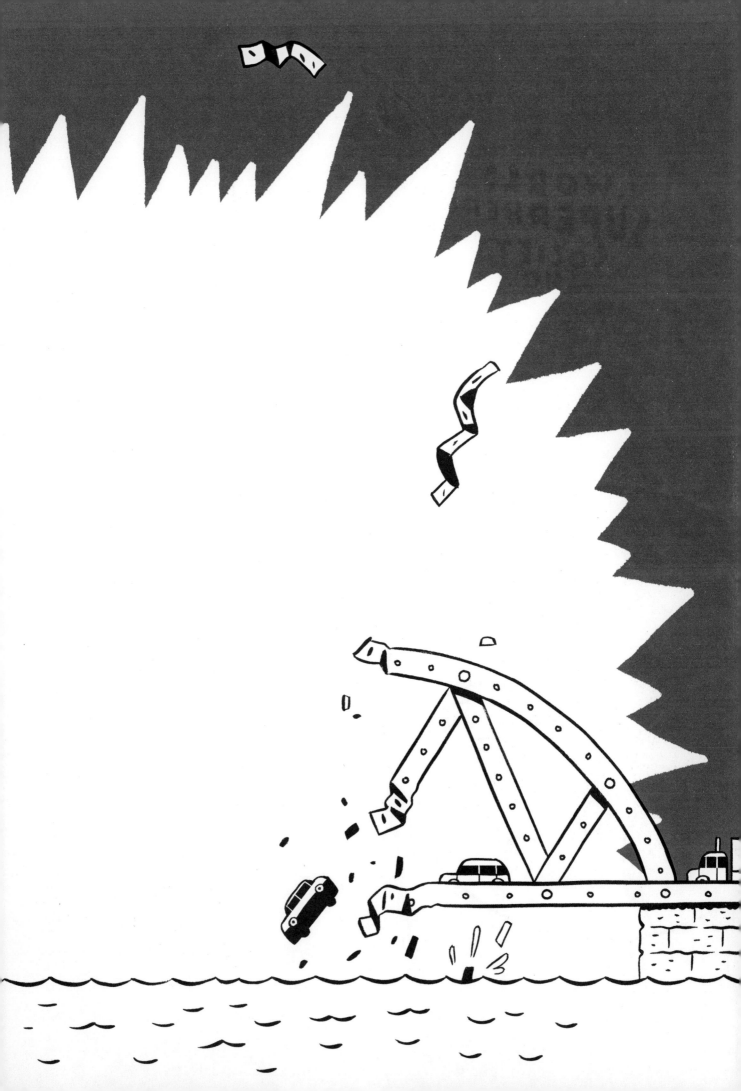

ALL THE HEROES HAVE
ASSEMBLED AT THE

WORLD SUPERHERO SOCIETY H.Q.

A SPACE STATION FLOATING ABOVE THE EARTH.

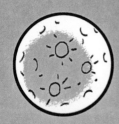

DRAW A COOL-LOOKING
CELESTIAL BASE.

WORLD SUPERHERO SOCIETY

CODE of CONDUCT

I _____

HEREBY SWEAR UNSWERVING ALLEGIANCE TO THE CODE OF CONDUCT BY WHICH ALL SUPERHEROES MUST ABIDE...

✳ TO FIGHT WRONG-DOING AND INJUSTICE WHEREVER THEY MAY LURK.

✳ TO APPREHEND AND VANQUISH THE PERPETRATORS.

✳ TO UPHOLD STRENGTH, COURAGE, AND JUSTICE.

✳ TO BE EVER VIGILANT AND TO KEEP MY NOSE AND OUTFIT CLEAN AT ALL TIMES.

SIGNED _____   DATE _____

ACKNOWLEDGMENTS

MEHALA FOR LOVE & SUPPORT

LAURENCE KING
ANGUS HYLAND
DONALD DINWIDDIE
JASON GODFREY
JO LIGHTFOOT
SRIJANA GURUNG
JENNY JACOBY
ANA GRAVE
TOM GAULD
DAN ADAMS
IAN WRIGHT
HAMISH & ALEXANDER

THANKYOU FOR ALL YOUR SUPPORT
& HARD WORK TO

DARREL, HELEN, AMANDA,
CHLOE & JENNY AT HEART

WWW. HEARTAGENCY. COM